Praise for *THE KEY*

...ss Leaders

"The Key tells the story of networking with clear and relevant examples of how to actually build long-term relationships in a modern service business. All business is personal and nothing is more important than developing strong relationships in navigating up the business hierarchy especially for professional women. Now there is an excellent guide book. I have known Ken for years and he is a true expert who has earned the right to author a book on networking. A must read!"

Sarah J. "Sally" Anderson, CPA
Chair of the Board, Pacific Symphony
Member, California Board of Accountancy
Retired Ernst & Young partner

"I have worked alongside Ken for 6 years. He brings new meaning to the word "Networking". While many associate networking with going out and shaking hands, Ken has taken this art to a science. In his book he has a step by step, easy to follow guide that could help both introverts and extroverts build human capital. His suggestions on how to incorporate the personal touch, with technology and good old fashioned handwritten notes, are simple and very effective. I have both seen and experienced it."

Lorraine Moos
EVP and Senior Partner
Project Pro Search

"I have known Ken Tudhope for 25 years since we were entry-level sales representatives in Procter & Gamble. In spite of living in 5 different countries over the course of my career, Ken always kept in touch with me and made me feel special including personal birthday cards (not emails!). His attention to detail and the little things that drive networking, relationships and keeping you in touch is exemplary leadership. I'm a huge fan and recommend him and this book without any reservation!"

Jeff D. Davis
President & CEO
Orabrush Inc.

"At Ingram Micro we always say it's about the people. As the world's largest technology distributor our role is to enable all our partners in the technology ecosystem. Interpersonal relationships are vital to smooth and successful operations. *The Key*, written by a true networking expert, is a simple, but powerful story about how anyone can build a valuable network with a very small investment of time or money."

Keith Bradley
President
Ingram Micro North America

"Our students at California State University Fullerton are blessed to have Ken Tudhope as a speaker each semester and I am confident that through his book more students will utilize the techniques he has perfected over his professional life. The book is well written and I believe will become an essential reading for all who try to establish effective communication links in today's complex business world."

Mohsen Sharifi, Ph.D., CMA
Department of Accounting
Mihaylo College of Business and Economics
California State University, Fullerton

"I recommend this book to anyone that wants to expand their network. Ken's engaging storytelling provides an easy to follow process no matter where you are in your career. His practical advice is powerful and yet simple to understand."

Kristin Walle
Vice President of Finance
ADP Tax and Financial Services

"*The Key* is the *How to Win Friends and Influence People* of our time. Delivered in a thoroughly entertaining narrative, Ken Tudhope elegantly delivers a simple yet profound message all professionals will find beneficial. Buy it for your children. Read it for yourself."

Ken Gryske
President
Spero Strategies LLC
Author of *The Hover Trap*

"Ken Tudhope is an expert networker who has built a successful business through developing relationships, while still serving clients. In *The Key*, Ken has taken this experience and distilled his natural ability into a process which any person can implement regardless of age, level or profession. *The Key* follows the career of a young CPA who recognizes that the key to building a successful career is through building a network – and she has a lot of fun doing it."

Melissa Griffiths
Principal
Active Advisors, Inc.

"I strongly recommend this book on networking by Ken Tudhope to professionals in both the public and private sectors. The art of networking is essential practice for a person in a leadership position and the strategies outlined by Ken are practical, easy to accomplish and they really make sense. Ken is quite successful because he truly believes in cultivating strong and lasting relationships with people. He has employed the concepts he describes in this work for many years and as a result he has established a large group of people who are true colleagues."

Frank "Jake" Abbott Ed. D.
Superintendent
California Public Schools

"Ken is the All-Star of Networking in my book and *The Key* is a fantastic, realistic depiction of how easy it can be. Times have changed and a robust network is a must in 2012. If you don't have one or your network could use a boost - read this book! Ken demonstrates the value of deliberate and intentional baby steps that make networking easy and effortless. Turning connections into relationships is magical and carries deep professional <u>and</u> personal rewards. I love his choice of characters which demonstrates that networking has equal opportunity and reward for both men and women. A must read!"

Kimberly Roush
Founder, KPMG MS All Stars!
Owner, All-Star Executive Coaching
Business Development, WOMEN Unlimited, Inc.

"The reason Ken is successful is not just because he 'gets it', but because he so genuinely cares about people. He sincerely looks out for other people every day and it is that caring and sincerity that has moved him forward in his various careers and it is the quality that comes out so beautifully in this book."

Terry Goldfarb-Lee
Senior Director of Business Development
Resources Global Professionals

"In his book *The Key*, Ken Tudhope makes a very clear case for the true value of having a strong network. He provides valuable insight in what little is needed to start building a network, maintaining and expanding it. His insights are as important to an engineer in the engineering, procurement and construction industry as they are in the accounting business and will for sure work in Europe as well as in the United States. I have seen through many personal cards, emails, etc. over many years that Ken Tudhope does exactly what he writes about in his book."

Marc van Heyningen
Vice President & General Manager The Netherlands
Fluor Corporation

THE KEY

A Networking Guide to
Meeting, Connecting and Succeeding

by

Ken Tudhope

www.networkingnote.com

THE KEY

Published by Kenneth A. Tudhope CPA, CMA, CGMA, MBA
Irvine, CA 92612

© 2012 Kenneth A. Tudhope
All rights reserved

First edition printed May 2012

ISBN: 9781477496152

Printed in the United States of America
By Create Space

This is a work of fiction. The ideas presented are those of the author alone. All references to possible results to be gained from the techniques discussed in this book relate to specific past examples and are not necessarily representative of any future results specific individuals may achieve.

TABLE OF CONTENTS

DEDICATION

To the networkers who see past the urgent demands of the day in order to connect with the people who have the ability to help make their lives rich.

ACKNOWLEGEMENTS

First and foremost, I have to thank my wife Jill who is my soul mate, business partner and editor. Her support enables me to excel. She is definitely the best writer I know and always makes my ideas sound better. This book would not have been possible without her and for her help I am eternally grateful.

Lorraine Moos is interesting, inspiring and the best friend and business partner I could imagine. She is smart, charismatic, confident, hardworking and fun to be around for 10 or 12 hours a day. She both inspires me and at the same time keeps me grounded. Truly, one of a kind!

I am so thankful to all the networking experts I have learned from: Harvey Mackay, Jeffrey Gitomer, Wayne Baker, Terry Goldfarb-Lee, Keith Ferrazzi, Dale Carnegie, Zig Ziglar, Darrell Gurney, Bill Ellermeyer, et. al. I devour their books, tapes and great ideas.

Dr. Moshin "Mo" Sharifi first invited me to speak about networking at California State University Fullerton. Mo connects academia to the business community and it has a great positive impact on our profession. I speak at many schools, but the accounting program at CSUF is the best, a true "Top West Coast University." It is my relationship with CSUF that gives me the examples to write this story.

The Board and the Members of the Orange County Chapters of Financial Executives International (FEI) and the Institute of Management Accountants (IMA) have given me an awesome place to network and helped me to realize every benefit possible from networking.

I would like to give huge thanks to Ken Gryske who is the catalyst that enabled me to finish this book and get it published. Ken is an executive coach and author of "The Hover Trap." He sure coached me get out of my "I almost have a book" hover trap.

At 43 years old, I left a corporate career with a steady paycheck and perceive security to start a new career in recruiting with only a few Rolodexes®. Since making this transition, I have built a successful business and sold more than $10 million in search and consulting services. I truly know the value of a powerful network. Thanks to Alan Boeckmann, the Chairman and CEO at Fluor who made the decision to move my job to Texas, and even a bigger thanks to Michael Dugan, Michael Hughes and all of my other friends who helped me after he did!

Thanks to all of my friends and supporters, I hope you enjoy this book and let's stay in touch.

Sincerely,

Ken

PREFACE

There is no reason to wait, NOW is the time to start networking.

Every year millions of people enter the professional work force. Fresh faces from colleges and universities throughout the world prepared to get started in their new careers. They are bright and positive; new professionals who feel entitled to success because they have an education. Starting at the bottom of their chosen profession, they are eager for career advancement.

Most assume their managers and some objective evaluation system will look out for them during their career progression. These new professionals believe if they put their heads down and work hard, career advancement will just happen. The best go to work early, stay late and give everything they have to their job.

No doubt, effort and education are two great cornerstones on which to build a career, but over time most professionals realize that actualizing success requires something more.

Hard work is a great start; for top students it has always worked in the past. Unfortunately this is the working world where current contributions trump past accomplishments, and there is no perfectly objective system of evaluation. Most new professionals begin to sense the political nature of the working world and sooner or later they hear someone say, "It's not *what* you know, but *who* you know that really matters."

Most reject this idea as blasphemous and don't give a second thought to the importance of relationships in their career advancement. They see very few immediate benefits in connecting with the people who can help them succeed in this strange new world of work.

At some point, however, all smart professionals realize that success is a people business, and while hard work and education are a great start, they certainly don't guarantee success. Career success requires the help of others. This book is meant to highlight the value of relationships to new professionals, and convince them that networking is the key to success in the professional world.

The KEY: A Networking Guide to Meeting, Connecting and Succeeding is the first networking guide focused entirely on new professionals. This book is unique because almost all material regarding networking is focused on mid-career professionals and executives with the resources, budgets and organizational influence that new professionals simply don't have.

For years, I have visited local businesses and universities speaking about the value of networking and how to do it. Only recently, however, I began to realize that even if people accept the importance of networking, they still have trouble understanding exactly how it would work in their lives. *The KEY* illustrates networking by telling the success story of a young woman who could be any new professional.

I hope it will illustrate and motivate. Most importantly, I hope it will teach readers just how simple and inexpensive it can be to build valuable relationships. My hope is that readers will give networking a serious try, because when they do, they will discover a *KEY* that will open many doors throughout their careers.

Good Luck and Good Networking!

Ken Tudhope CPA, CMA, CGMA
CEO, Project Pro Search
"Connected. So We Can Connect You"

FOREWORD

If you don't know Ken, you don't know networking. It's an honor and a privilege to be asked by Ken Tudhope to open his book with a Foreword. And the foremost word in Ken Tudhope's mind, body and soul is *networking*.

At the time of the writing of this Foreword, Ken Tudhope has amassed more than 1,500 networking lunches since 2006. That adds up to Ken being at a networking lunch on more than 92% of all work days! That's an impressive statistic.

How many of us could profess to spend more than 92% of our lunches in front of someone we know professionally for the simple intent to get to know them better and for them to know us better? Of course, there are other benefits that come out of such a practice: more business, deeper relationships, inside information, expanded referrals, good ideas, etc. Yet, those are simply all the gravy goodies that fall out of merely having interest in people and getting in front of them to express that interest on a regular basis.

I've written on networking. I've trained many an executive on networking. I've seen miracles come about, both personally and professionally, in my life and the lives of others through relationships. And there isn't a new grad or even seasoned executive on the planet that can't benefit in untold ways from the power of networking.

Ken has taken the time to spell out for each and every young professional exactly how and why networking is the first and foremost key to building a successful professional career. Networking is far more important to a new professional, because effective networking will get a new grad in front of decision makers who can open doors. As the old saying states, "It's not what you know, it's who you know…and who knows you."

You see, all seasoned executives—which most new grads want to become—understand the omnipotence of networking. So, when they see networking properly implemented and demonstrated by a younger professional, it catches their attention. And that's what you always want to do: catch positive attention.

No doubt, consistent networking is probably the single best "Key", as Ken calls it, to take your career wherever you want it to go. Even entire career changes can be accomplished through networking that could never happen through a traditional, "front door" approach. People bend rules for people that they know…and people simply like to work with people they like.

I believe every young person should have *The Key* in their pocket not only when they are graduating from years of college preparation for that "real" world, but also in their pocket even on Day 1 of their matriculation. That network built while still in college can be one of the best to maintain as the years go by. While *The Key* is a great resource for students, it is also a great resource for seasoned executives as they consider the benefits of a networking tune-up.

We tap into *The Key* through the allegory of a young, new professional with neither budgets nor organizational power: direct from her eyes, mind, beliefs and habits. We watch as she matures and grows, to work her network for ever increasing benefits. No overnight success stories, but we marvel as she manifests career moves only possible through connections. We laugh as she justifies using the old fashioned Rolodex® "front and center" on her desk in the age of invisible-throughout-the-day "friends" on social media. And we delight as she discovers that the actual value of her connections exceeds far beyond even the monetary value that Ken suggests.

It's time that business and other schools take on a greater responsibility to ensure that graduates learn the grease of the working world that keeps the career gears turning…and I challenge every new grad to get this book and learn networking yourself if your school isn't getting the job done. And trust me…for the most part they're not.

Darrell W. Gurney
Founder of CareerGuy.com and author of
Never Apply for a Job Again: Break the Rules, Cut the Line, Beat the Rest and *Headhunters Revealed! Career Secrets for Choosing and Using Professional Recruiters*

The Decision to Invest in Relationships:

• • •

It is said that a journey of 1,000 miles starts with but a single step. Connecting with people is a huge opportunity open to all of us. Networking requires neither a budget nor a title and is as valuable to a college student or recent graduate as it is to a corporate executive or partner in an accounting firm. These relationships create social capital that is as valuable as financial capital or intellectual capital. Social capital is a leveraged form of human capital with truly limitless potential for those who work at it. Now is the best time to begin.

Ann was elated to have accepted the job offer from one of the large, international, "Big-4" accounting firms. It was the perfect "next step" in her accounting career which began four years earlier with her decision to become an accounting major at a top west coast university. The job in the Big-4 had huge potential, but would start out with an incredibly demanding schedule of 60+ hour work weeks and preparation for the CPA exam on top of that.

Ann was a gifted student who had been number one in her class in the accounting program (she also had a minor in International Business and Asian Studies). In addition to academics, she had become increasingly involved in extracurricular activities in the Accounting Department, although in the beginning she didn't really know why. She did it because all the other top students did it and she had never shied away from hard work and challenge.

It took only one "all hands" office meeting to realize there were few partners who looked much like Ann.

Even with this excellent academic resume, Ann was a bit nervous about a job in the Big-4. She knew her colleagues would all be the best of the best, and sensed career success would require much more than pure intelligence and hard work which had enabled her to excel in school.

Nobody talked openly about it, but as an Asian woman born outside the United States, there were further challenges. It took only one "all hands" office meeting to realize there were few partners who looked much like Ann. No doubt, her new employer was a successful partnership led by people and she would probably need to be extra-special to be invited into the "club" by the "old boys' network."

Looking back, Ann realized the KEY to receiving multiple job offers from Big-4, regional and local CPA firms centered on the year she was president of her university's chapter of the accounting academic honor society called Beta Alpha Psi (BAP). See Appendix -3 for more information about Beta Alpha Psi. It enabled her to make deep relationships with all the top accounting students (graduate and undergraduate) and also gave her significant exposure to the people in the top accounting firms she knew she would be targeting in her job search. She sensed the value of these relationships and didn't want to let them go even though most of the

"Who you know and who knows you is the KEY to long-term career success."
~Ken

professionals she met were very busy and scattered throughout the 10 - 15 firms who actively recruited on campus.

What's more, once she accepted the job offer from her firm, most of her professional contacts had no obvious reason to stay in touch with her. As busy professionals and potential competitors they quickly began to fade away. Ann's motivation to act grew as she heard the voice of Ken Tudhope reverberating in her head, "who you know and who knows you is the KEY to long term career success."

Ken is a fanatic! He's a networking expert who was invited by the Beta Alpha Psi chapter to come to the university each semester to evangelize on the importance of building relationships in business. Over the years, Ken has "earned" the spot as the speaker at the first meeting of each semester which always has the highest attendance. A Big- 4 CPA himself (PricewaterhouseCoopers), Ken passionately advocates networking as the KEY to professional, corporate and entrepreneurial success.

Each fall and spring during his presentations, Ken carries his is five or six Rolodexes® to the podium. Filled with business cards, Ken would hold them up and claim they were absolutely his most valuable assets. He not at all bothered by the fact that many of the students thought his Rolodexes® were an anachronism in the modern era of Google, LinkedIn and Facebook.

By graduation, Ann had seen Ken speak about networking more than six times and his message was indelibly planted in her mind. She actually began to look forward to his stories about the value of networking and liked his optimistic opinion of the future for those with quality contacts. His talks were interesting and entertaining, exactly opposite of the dull, technical speeches delivered by the "suits" from the accounting firms.

The KEY to receiving more help, opportunities, good ideas and resources, is to make more friends and develop good ways of staying in touch.

Ken would enthusiastically tell the students about the value of contacts and the things he did to create and maintain his significant professional network. By far, he gave the best advice about how to connect with the recruiting contacts and the other professionals from the accounting firms the students so eagerly wanted to work at. Ann sensed these connections would be critical to her success even though most students and professionals leave them behind when work begins. Ken's ideas and methods were simple and actually made the recruiting process fun and interesting.

Ken put a value of approximately $50 on each connection and used the enterprise value of Facebook, LinkedIn and even an offer he received for his own business to prove it. Ann wasn't exactly sure about his calculations, but got Ken's message loud and clear about the real value of positive relationships. The KEY to receiving more help, opportunities, good ideas and resources, is to make more friends and to develop effective ways of staying in touch.

> *Ken's advice for networking through groups: sign up, show up, follow up and step up.*

The main message was that people don't have to go it alone. Even students and newly minted professionals at the lowest end of the corporate or professionals services hierarchy can build large, valuable networks. With a little bit of consistent effort and an attitude of giving first, anyone can receive valuable help and opportunities through networking. Ken's enthusiasm and encouragement for students to step up into leadership roles in student groups was also a large part of the reason Ann decided to run for Beta Alpha Psi (BAP) President during the second semester of her junior year.

At Beta Alpha Psi, Ann took Ken's advice for networking through groups: sign-up, show up, follow up and step up. She had long since signed up because Beta Alpha Psi is known as a high-quality organization that attracts the best accounting students and the top recruiters. Beta Alpha Psi requires members to show up to events and meetings. Ann had already stepped up to a position on the Board and ultimately won the election to become President. The only thing left was to develop the habit of consistent follow up.

During her presidency she began the practice of following up with all the professionals she met at BAP meetings, social activities and recruiting events. Most students didn't do anything, but those who did follow-up usually sent emails. Ann wanted to be a little bit different and memorable so she decided to follow up in person by placing a telephone call to each and every professional that came to the campus.

It was the phone call that mattered -- not what she said -- and the reason was that no other student did it consistently.

Her system was simple. She asked for business cards from the guests. When she got them, she immediately put them together in her wallet where they would not be misplaced. Never being more than about 10 professionals at a single event, it wasn't difficult to manage.

She realized she the follow up just required a process and a bit of discipline; it soon became a habit. The day after each Beta Alpha Psi event, she would get up early and make calls from her desk. Once a call was made the card was moved from her wallet to the top drawer in her desk.

The calls took less than 5 minutes total because most of them went to voicemail. Either way, she briefly thanked the professionals for their time and quickly got off the line. Ann felt like she needed to keep talking but soon learned that "less is more." It was the call that mattered not what she said, and the reason was that no other student did it consistently. At first it felt funny calling people she barely knew, but soon she got better at small talk and the calls became second nature.

Every now and then, a conversation ensued and once even led to a coffee meeting with a female professional in the Big-4 who was a past president of Beta Alpha Psi. Once she got into it, Ann realized calling didn't require much time and the professionals seemed to appreciate it. Before long, they began to look for her at events and even greeted her by name from memory.

Thinking back, she smiled when remembering the amusing story Ken told about his friend from

PricewaterhouseCoopers who said, "Our recruiting team simply endorsed the people we liked."

At the time, Ann mistakenly assumed that there was some sophisticated evaluation process going on behind the scenes. When actually the busy professionals only had time enough to report who they liked and didn't like (which worked because membership in Beta Alpha Psi had already vetted the students academically and the Beta Alpha Psi leadership hierarchy was a good indicator of drive and ambition). Of course there is an official hiring system, but when faced with a multitude of great candidates, "who they like" is always the tie breaker.

Ann was sure that the KEY to being liked and remembered by these extremely busy professionals was her follow-up.

In the end, Ann was sure that the KEY to being remembered by these extremely busy professionals was her follow-up. At some point during the recruiting process,

Ann consciously decided to make every effort to stay in touch with these valuable contacts *forever*; regardless of the demands of her new job and profession.

KEY Questions:

1. What types of people did Ann have access to at this time?

2. Who did Ann connect with and what did she do to connect with them?

3. What was her cost of networking, e.g. time, money, opportunity costs, etc.?

4. What were the benefits of networking, e.g., tangible, intangible, monetary, ideas, information, etc.?

5. Besides Ann, who was actively networking in the story? What did they do? How did they benefit?

6. Who are the good networkers where you are? What can you do better to connect with people where you are now? What is stopping you from accessing the Key?

Managing Contact Information:

• • •

Social media and e-mail make it possible to reach almost anyone on the earth in an instant. The challenge is most people don't save or organize the contact information from the people they meet. Business cards are lost, group rosters and directories are left behind, names and faces are forgotten. Organizing and storing contact information is the first step to staying in touch. It just takes commitment, desktop software which most professionals already have and a small amount of time.

• • •

ne of the things she did while wrapping-up her college career was to create a list of the people she met along the way. Ann didn't have money to buy a fancy contact relationship management program so she started with Microsoft Excel. One Sunday afternoon she took some time and began to create a list.

The students were easy; she had the BAP and Accounting Society rosters from her junior and senior years already in Excel. She got the names and contact information for the two accounting professors she liked the most and added them to the list. She really liked Dr. Tang.

He was a great guy who was originally from China and in addition to teaching, was the faculty liaison to Beta Alpha Psi and a member of Financial Executives International (FEI) and the Institute of Management Accountants (IMA). She spent a considerable amount of time with him as she became increasingly involved in Beta Alpha Psi leadership. Dr. Tang was a great networker himself who has built a valuable bridge between the University and the local business community.

Classification was KEY to differentiating people she hardly knew, and might soon forget.

The professionals were a bit tougher since she had not done a great job filing all the business cards she had collected over the years. It didn't take long however to find about 50 business cards scattered in her desk drawer. Inputting the contact information into Excel was another story, she wondered if it was worth all the tedious work but she did it anyway.

The student contacts were distinguishable from professionals and professors in her Excel list because the title cell was empty for most of the. She made the decision to enter "student" as the title for her classmates until she found out where they were working. She added a column she titled "reminder" and wrote a few words that would help her remember the person, e.g., what they looked like, their role in BAP or Accounting Society, their hometown, etc. This activity made Ann realize that accurate and detailed personal information is KEY to differentiating people she hardly knew and would soon forget.

The Excel list now had over 300 names including some people she knew well and others she didn't know at all. The whole exercise took a few hours. She did most of it while "watching" her favorite movie, one she had seen many, many times before.

According to the $50 per connection valuation, her Excel list was worth approximately $15,000. If this valuation was anywhere near correct, at that time, the list was the most valuable asset Ann possessed. To protect it she made a back-up copy and emailed it to her parents for safe keeping. Later she used DropBox to save a copy in a secure location. With cloud storage being readily accessible and mostly free, technology is helping new professionals on tight budgets now more than ever to protect valuable contact information over the years.

Her peers thought it was "old school", but she bought a Rolodex® file anyway and stapled the 50 or so business cards to paper Rolodex® insert cards, and filed them in her new Rolodex® file in alphabetical order by last name. When she finished she put it on her desk, front and center.

She knew one big KEY to networking was staying in touch, but in pulling the list together, Ann realized managing contact information would take some thought and effort. It felt good to, however, to know that she had assembled a solid list of personal emails and cell phone numbers for students, and work addresses, office phone numbers, and emails for the professors and professionals. She was also connected to many of these people on

Ann realized that managing contact information would take some thought and effort.

Facebook and others on LinkedIn.

Ann loved the holidays, but couldn't mail a card to the students if she didn't have a permanent mailing address. On the other hand, she thought it would be awkward to send a card to a professional she hadn't interacted with for a while. Would an email suffice? What would she write about? As time passes and people move, would she lose track of them? What would they have in common? After seeing the power of the Beta Alpha Psi network, she was committed, but not exactly sure what to do next as she entered the working world.

KEY Questions:

1. What types of people did Ann have access to at this time?

2. Who did Ann connect with and what did she do to connect with them?

3. What was her cost of networking, e.g. time, money, opportunity costs, etc.?

4. What were the benefits of networking, e.g., tangible, intangible, monetary, ideas, information, etc.?

5. Besides Ann, who was actively networking in the story? What did they do? How did they benefit?

6. Who are the good networkers where you are? What can you do better to connect with people where you are now? What is stopping you from accessing the Key?

Consistent Periodic Contact:

• • •

People in modern society are in constant motion and without proactive effort to stay in contact, relationships fade. Once a relationship is established, maintaining contact is more about the quantity and consistency of communication than the depth of each interaction. Make it easy for people to stay interested in what you are doing by announcing the significant milestones in your life. E-mail is the best method.

• • •

Ann decided to call Ken Tudhope. He encouraged and reminded her that any networking activity would be beneficial. He also reassured her, whatever she decided to do would put her way ahead of most of her peers who would do nothing to build and maintain a professional network even after their positive BAP experience. The KEY was to do *something*. He recommended she start by sending a short e-mail thanking the people who had helped her in college and announcing her new position.

The e-mail would be quick and simple. She used her Excel contact list and a basic mail merge or BCC. The message was short and included her new contact information. At the end of the message, she asked for the job status and updated contact information from the recipients, as well as extending an open invitation to use her as a resource.

The message was written in such a way it was appropriate to be sent to everyone on her list: friends, family, students, professionals, etc. It hadn't taken long to write and with a press of a button the message was off.

She even received replies from professionals at a firm where she turned down a job offer.

A few of the e-mails bounced, but almost all the messages got through. Ann was surprised so many people replied. She even received replies from professionals at firms where she turned down job offers. A significant side-benefit was that she no longer felt bad for not accepting the competing offers from the professionals she befriended during the recruiting process.

She was amazed when two people she could barely remember responded with congratulations as if they were her best friends, and she began to understand what was meant by "Who knows you?"

Ann made sure to review each e-mail signature in the replies to ensure nothing had changed, e.g. address, title, phone number, etc. In some cases it had been a long time since she had obtained the contact information, and in a few cases there were changes that required updating in her contact list.

KEY Questions:

1. What types of people did Ann have access to at this time?

2. Who did Ann connect with and what did she do to connect with them?

3. What was her cost of networking, e.g. time, money, opportunity costs, etc.?

4. What were the benefits of networking, e.g., tangible, intangible, monetary, ideas, information, etc.?

5. Besides Ann, who was actively networking in the story? What did they do? How did they benefit?

6. Who are the good networkers where you are? What can you do better to connect with people where you are now? What is stopping you from accessing the Key?

Years 1 - 3: Work Hard but Don't Disappear

•   •   •

Most professionals simply disappear in the first few years of their career. They put their heads down and work like crazy. Good start, but it's not enough. Hard work can only build a foundation; relationships attract the opportunity that sits on top of that foundation. Networking takes consistency and commitment but not a lot of time or money. Obtaining business cards is basic, recording contact information is a good idea; using the information to connect is smart, valuable, and KEY to career success.

•   •   •

As she expected, work was very demanding and there was absolutely zero time for formal networking. In her first year, however, she decided to take two baby steps: first, she committed to carrying her own business cards and using them to get the cards of the people she met in business; second, she decided to send holiday messages. The KEY was to find efficient ways to stay in front of people even when she was super busy.

Ken had always said the best way to get someone's business card is to offer yours and in her first year Ann was never without her business cards. They became her most prized accessory. For example, when Ann took a CPA review course, she was all business in preparing for the exam. When she met someone new in the prep class she offered her card and always asked for the other person's card. Frankly, she was amazed by how few of these service professionals (her peers) ever carried business cards.

The KEY was to find efficient ways to stay in front of people, even when Ann was super busy.

At the time, Ann didn't even realize that connecting with people in the profession was becoming an ingrained habit.

The contact information went into the computer (she had now uploaded her Excel list to MS Outlook) and she placed the card into her Rolodex® file on her desk (still front and center). She was so busy at the holidays that she decided to send hand-written cards to only about 25 important contacts (mostly family members, friends, former BAP board Colleagues, alumni, and peers at the firm).

She sent an e-mail to the rest of her list thanking them for their support, and wishing them a happy holiday season and best wishes for the New Year.

Her second and third years were just as busy at work, but she successfully passed the CPA exam which freed up some time. This was a great accomplishment and she used the occasion to send out a short e-mail announcement.

The KEY at this time in her career was not to lose touch with people.

For Ann, it honestly felt very awkward announcing her success. Ann's family was traditional Chinese and they believed in letting hard work and results speak for themselves. Ann decided to send the announcement anyway and was glad she did. At the bottom of the e-mail message she asked for updated contact information and received quite a few responses. Her contacts were mostly new in their careers and there was significant movement.

The KEY at this time in her career was not to lose touch with people.

She was amazed by how many congratulatory e-mails she received from the professionals she met during her BAP Presidency; these people were beginning to feel like old friends. Again, she also received responses from people she could barely remember. Ann was a bit embarrassed for not remembering them, but rather than fading away, she used it as a good reminder to reconnect, and in several cases used this as motivation to pictures and profiles on LinkedIn.

The KEY to networking at this point was persistence.

Fellow alumni from her accounting program took this occasion to congratulate Ann on her success and updated her on their situation. Each time one of them passed the CPA exam, Ann sent a congratulatory card to them. She felt a hand-written message separated her from the e-mail crowd and was glad she had been careful to record mailing addresses for several years.

Again, she sent mostly holiday e-mails and didn't attend any formal networking events. She did, however, volunteer to be on her firm's recruiting team at her alma mater and bumped into Dr. Tang once or twice a year, which she enjoyed greatly. Recruiting was fun because she could see how far she had grown, but was also beneficial in another way: it gave Ann the ability to meet the new staff and learn which ones she should request for her jobs and clients.

Unfortunately, even though networking was becoming a habit, Ann was beginning to have questions and concerns. She worked so hard at her job, and just surviving in the Big-4 was all consuming. Any additional work activities layered on top of that were extremely difficult. So far it seemed that Ann was networking with an attitude of "give first, expect nothing" and all that, but it had now been almost 4 years and to date, there had been only a few tangible benefits from all her efforts. Nonetheless, Ann could see that the most successful people in the firm and at client companies were all well connected, so she decided stay at it. The KEY to networking at this point was persistence and consistency.

KEY Questions:

1. What types of people did Ann have access to at this time?

2. Who did Ann connect with and what did she do to connect with them?

3. What was her cost of networking, e.g. time, money, opportunity costs, etc.?

4. What were the benefits of networking, e.g., tangible, intangible, monetary, ideas, information, etc.?

5. Besides Ann, who was actively networking in the story? What did they do? How did they benefit?

6. Who are the good networkers where you are? What can you do better to connect with people where you are now? What is stopping you from accessing the Key?

Year 4: The Network Comes Alive

* * *

Success takes time. Networking takes consistency, generosity, and faith. When we "give often and expect nothing" good things happen. Most companies have a target charity and the supporting activities are usually sponsored by top executives. Taking advantage of these activities is a great way to build relationships not normally available to new professionals in any other way. In time, social capital pays big dividends, but it takes work, patience and consistency; most people give up before the dividends pay out.

* * *

At the beginning of Ann's fourth year she was promoted to Senior Auditor, so she sent another message announcing this job promotion to her network of contacts. Like all the previous announcements, the process was the same and by now she getting much more efficient. This time the responses resulted in one noticeable difference: her contacts outside the firm began inquiring about her career plans and implied they could help her when she was ready for a move. She was happy in her job and was certainly not looking for a new one, but it sure felt nice to know there was opportunity waiting and her friends were looking out for her.

Ann wasn't actually an extrovert, but she was becoming known as a bit of a connector with the people in her office.

She continued to ask for business cards from the people she met, which wasn't difficult given the fact she served so many different clients. Ann noticed she was about to fill up her first Rolodex® card file and celebrated when she purchased the second one. They both sat prominently on her desk at work in full view of everyone in the office. Ann liked the way it looked and besides, they reminded her to keep networking. If Rolodex® files were "old school," and Google, Facebook and LinkedIn were "new school," then in this high-tech / high-touch business world, she thought the combination of the two should be called "smart-school."

Ann wasn't actually an extrovert, but she was becoming known as a bit of a connector with the people in her office. That year she was invited by several of the managers and partners to ride on the MS All-Stars cycling team to raise money for Multiple Sclerosis. MS was a top national charity for the firm and a popular event in her local office. Ann didn't sign up at first for several reasons: she was busy at work, she wasn't in very good shape, she didn't think she could raise money, and she simply wasn't an athlete. However, her schedule slowed a bit that fall and she went to lunch with Ken Tudhope.

At lunch she mentioned the MS ride and was surprised to find Ken was riding on the team! Members of the team don't have to be firm employees and Ken had been invited by the former partner who actually founded the MS All-Stars. Ken highly encouraged Ann to join the team. "It's a good cause," he advised, "it's great networking, and good for your health."

It wasn't too late so Ann signed up and reluctantly agreed to the $400 minimum for fundraising. On weekends in the fall, Ann did training rides with partners, managers, peers, clients, Ken, and others. She learned things about the firm she didn't know, some of which was quite surprising (Ann thought it was great she was now somewhat on the "inside"), and one Partner even invited

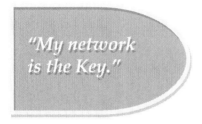

her to lunch to discuss her career development goals and how he could help. Ken Tudhope went on-and-on about the value of networking.

Relationships deepened and it made going to work every day even more enjoyable. Several members of the All Star team were firm alumni who were now in Controllership positions in local companies. With hours in the saddle riding next to them and talking, Ann learned what it's like on the other side of the audit equation. This knowledge made her more efficient in her audit work and much better at client relations. In addition, there was a fellow she was interested in and invited him to be a member of the team. Ann was thrilled when he said yes.

To raise money for MS through the All-star team, Ann sent an e-mail to her contact list (now over 400) with the same basic format as her prior announcements and was amazed at the response. Messages of encouragement with small donations flowed in from many people including: past BAP Board colleagues, alumni, co-workers, clients, friends and family, and she quickly exceeded the minimum required donation and ultimately Ann rose to near the top of the office's fund raiser list.

The Partner who was team captain took notice and stopped by her cube to acknowledge her contributions. When she asked Ann how she did it, Ann simply pointed at the Rolodexes® on her desk, smiled and said, "My network is the Key." Ann touched her network again by sending a hand-written thank-you note to all of the people who donated to her ride. She also stopped by the office of the Partner who was the MS All-Stars team captain and thanked him for his leadership and committed to riding for the All-Star team the following year.

KEY Questions:

1. What types of people did Ann have access to at this time?

2. Who did Ann connect with and what did she do to connect with them?

3. What was her cost of networking, e.g. time, money, opportunity costs, etc.?

4. What were the benefits of networking, e.g., tangible, intangible, monetary, ideas, information, etc.?

5. Besides Ann, who was actively networking in the story? What did they do? How did they benefit?

6. Who are the good networkers where you are? What can you do better to connect with people where you are now? What is stopping you from accessing the Key?

Year 5: Networking Has Valuable Career Impact

● ● ●

We often hear the saying, "It's not what you know, but rather who you know that really matters." In business it is really "Who knows you." When we build a large network, even people we don't know very well start to remember and support us. Because of this, the benefits of networking often come in areas we are not actively focused on or expecting.

● ● ●

In her fifth year at the firm Ann was getting good at networking. She was still too busy to be out at networking events, but she was always careful to get people's business cards and follow up. She found a way to send an announcement or two throughout the year and was up to about 75 hand-written holiday cards.

It was during this year she also co-captained the MS All-Stars. She was becoming quite comfortable working on the event with partners, managers and even the National

Office (the MS ride is a national charity event for the firm and Ann helped design their new MS All-Stars team jersey). When she sent her holiday cards, she now had strong enough relationships to send them to people up in the hierarchy, e.g. managers, partners, clients, in addition to her peers. It was nice to get cards in return and Ann was sure to record home addresses and spouses' names from the return address labels.

Periodic personalized communication over the years was the KEY.

Ann couldn't really announce it to her network, but she was so excited when one of her undergraduate colleagues from the BAP Board called her and asked her to bid on the annual audit and tax services for his family's sizable manufacturing business. Ann really had no idea how this was done. But after she left a voicemail for the Office Managing Partner regarding the opportunity, she got an immediate return call. The firm won the business and Ann received an unexpected cash bonus.

Frankly, Ann did not know the fellow who referred her to the opportunity very well when they were in school. She would have never guessed he'd be the one to bring her first sales opportunity. This reconfirmed the value of "Who knows you?" and when she thanked him, she asked why he had called her.

He replied, "You have always been a leader. I benefited from your work at Bata Alpha Psi and have enjoyed following your progress over the years. I knew you would not let us down." Funny she thought, in order for him to "follow" her, Ann had to send him her periodic announcements, holiday

Her excellent relationships with so many decision makers within the firm was KEY to obtaining a "get out of jail free" card.

messages and MS Ride e-mails. Periodic personalized communication over the years was the KEY.

That year there were lay-offs at the firm and fortunately Ann was not selected for termination. In fact, several of her friends in management positions put her at ease by telling her off-line that her position was not under consideration for downsizing. Ann had a strong work ethic, but only slightly above average technical skills in accounting and auditing. There was little doubt in her mind that her excellent relationships with so many decision makers within the firm were KEY to obtaining her "get out of jail free" card.

When word about the pending lay-offs at her firm hit the industry "grapevine", Ann received several unsolicited recruiting calls from people in her network all offering support, ideas and actual referrals to great jobs. Ann was confident that even if she *had* been terminated; she would have found her a new job very quickly. She realized then that her network of contacts would always be a great resource in any career transition.

KEY Questions:

1. What types of people did Ann have access to at this time?

2. Who did Ann connect with and what did she do to connect with them?

3. What was her cost of networking, e.g. time, money, opportunity costs, etc.?

4. What were the benefits of networking, e.g., tangible, intangible, monetary, ideas, information, etc.?

5. Besides Ann, who was actively networking in the story? What did they do? How did they benefit?

6. Who are the good networkers where you are? What can you do better to connect with people where you are now? What is stopping you from accessing the Key?

Joining Toastmasters® Develops Confidence and People Skills

• • •

Toastmasters International® is a dream come true for new professionals. The personal and professional development is unmatched and the cost is almost nothing. There are numerous clubs in communities all over the country meeting throughout the day and week. It is a structured program that develops people through public speaking. Speaking publically is absolutely debilitating for many people; delivering numerous talks at Toastmasters® meetings builds technique and confidence. Toastmasters® is a very supportive environment. By supporting others going through this self-development process, one builds empathy and interpersonal skills. For new professionals this can also be a great opportunity to learn to network through groups: Sign up, Show up, Follow up, and Step up.

• • •

Ann's family was originally from Taiwan and had only come to the US when Ann was in her teens. She always felt a little bit like an outsider and was concerned her accent and lack of knowledge of the native culture might hold her back. Lately she had turned down one or two opportunities to speak publically due to lack of confidence. She wanted to work on this perceived area of weakness. She heard Toastmasters® had a fantastic development program and remembered Ken highly recommending it. The early morning club met at the Community Center near her apartment. It was perfect for her busy schedule so she signed up and paid the nominal annual registration fee.

This improved her management skills and enhanced her ability to build client relationships.

Ann's progress in Toastmasters® was better than expected and in the following year she accepted a few speaking engagements at firm training events and client-facing seminars. When it was appropriate, Ann made sure to invite a few of her contacts to each speaking activity. Very few accepted, but they all appreciated the invitation, and additionally, the invitations helped remind them what Ann was up to.

Ann found three other hidden benefits of Toastmasters®. First, by seeing the courage it took some people to speak before the group and the positive and encouraging way people in Toastmasters® responded to them, Ann learned deep empathy. Goodness knows she was afraid in delivering those first few speeches and so appreciated the support of the other members of the group.

As she became more confident she was able to help and support others through the process and over time she became a better people person. This improved her management skills and enhanced her ability to build client relationships.

Ann found the KEY to successfully building relationships required her to overcome her fear and master the art of public speaking.

Second, by listening to so many speeches she got an advanced lesson in US culture and developed conversational knowledge on a wide variety of subjects. When there were topics or issues she simply didn't understand, she found Toastmasters® a safe place to ask for clarification. It was through a friend at Toastmasters® that she developed the ability to talk "football." She never felt comfortable asking these types of questions at work or back when she was in school and her family simply didn't have enough experience in the US to teach her.

Finally, she met a diverse group of people and through a referral from a member of the club, found an opportunity that brought more paying work to her firm. She also met her soul mate and was married after a 14-month romance.

Ann found the KEY to successfully building relationships required her to build self-confidence, overcome the fear of strangers and to develop empathy and the ability to connect with a diverse set of people.

KEY Questions:

1. What types of people did Ann have access to at this time?

2. Who did Ann connect with and what did she do to connect with them?

3. What was her cost of networking, e.g. time, money, opportunity costs, etc.?

4. What were the benefits of networking, e.g., tangible, intangible, monetary, ideas, information, etc.?

5. Besides Ann, who was actively networking in the story? What did they do? How did they benefit?

6. Who are the good networkers where you are? What can you do better to connect with people where you are now? What is stopping you from accessing the Key?

Years 6 and 7: Networking Habits

● ● ●

Networking is not an event. It is a series of habits when consistently applied, create a way of life complete with many valuable and rewarding relationships. It is more art than science, but more often than not lunch meetings are a key way to connect. When people are away from the office they often relax; relationships grow deeper and friendships form.

● ● ●

I n years 6 and 7 her career progressed quite nicely. Ann was promoted to Manager on schedule and was able to add regular business lunches to her networking activities. The lunches were easy. She had watched Ken rack up big numbers of lunches on "Tudhope's Lunch Counter" at www.networkingnote.com and #kentudhope on Twitter.com. If he could go every day, why couldn't she go regularly, say once per week? Given the demands of the job, she never reached the one per week goal. However, it was a good goal and she grew steadily up to 35 or 40 networking lunches per year and *that* was significantly more than anyone else at her level in the firm.

She mostly invited clients and they almost always said yes. Ann always paid the tab; why not pay, she was being reimbursed by her employer. Once these lunches became a habit, she wondered why more professionals in the firm didn't take advantage of the reimbursed lunches.

Time together outside work affords the opportunity to build deeper relationships.

Most of her peers worked through lunch, but Ann realized that working at lunch only begets more work. On the other hand, a friendly business lunch begets more business and more friends. Time outside work affords the opportunity to build deeper relationships.

She was amazed at how these simple lunches improved her working relationships with clients and others. Ann found relationships got deeper when she spent time away from work one-on-one with clients and associates. When clients couldn't go, she called old friends from the BAP days or those who continually supported her MS ride (non-reimbursable but the lunches were another way to say thanks for the support). From time-to-time she'd even go to lunch with Ken Tudhope who had now become a friend and mentor.

> *She found the KEY to getting people to open up was asking good questions.*

At first she was afraid she wouldn't have anything to talk about at lunch. An hour can be a long time to spend with someone you don't know very well, but Ann learned people like to talk about themselves. She found the KEY to getting people to open up was asking good questions so she memorized a short list of questions like:

- ✓ What have you learned?
- ✓ What advice would you have?
- ✓ What is your favorite…?
- ✓ Where are you from?
- ✓ Tell me about your family?

The answers to these questions were Key to understanding the personal side of business colleagues. The more active she became, the easier it was, until she grew to really enjoyed these business lunches.

Once again, networking was the KEY to the firm winning the business and Ann earning a cash bonus.

Another funny thing happened, the speeches and stories that she had either delivered or heard in the Toastmasters® meetings constantly came back as a source of conversation. Ann realized that there were subtle and long-term interpersonal skills she developed through her experience in Toastmasters®. She was becoming a more interesting, well-rounded and knowledge person and this enables her to more easily connect with others.

She continued to send announcements, holiday cards and the annual MS ride letter to her network. There is no way her contacts could forget her and by this time some would say she was developing a personal brand of sorts.

Ann was amazed when twice; she was called for sales opportunities by the professionals from the small regional firms who had unsuccessfully recruited her in college.

In one case, a client had out-grown the regional CPA firm and needed to engage a Big-4 firm. In another case a client acquired a company in Europe and needed international transactions services the regional firm simply didn't provide. Once again, networking was the KEY to the firm winning the business and Ann earning a bonus.

In fact that year she earned more than now bonus. When several Senior Auditors abruptly resigned the Firm announced it would pay a $5,000 bonus to anyone who could successfully recruit experienced Senior Auditors to the firm. Ann reviewed he contacts list and realized that she knew many qualified people. She made some calls and within a few months 2 of her contacts had been hired. Her peers thought she was lucky, but Ann knew she was realizing some of the financial benefits of staying in touch with people in her profession.

At the same time, she regularly received calls for new job opportunities. Almost on a monthly basis she was called for a quality Assistant Controller position somewhere in Southern California through referrals from her network. She was now an audit Manager who was competent at her work and good with both employees and clients. The Partners in the office noticed and for project with high-profile clients. Ann was in high demand. With such positive relationships inside and outside the firm, she really enjoyed her work and felt a strong sense of loyalty to her colleagues and the firm. Work was fun and fulfilling.

Her trusted relationships were KEY to Ann becoming a hero of sorts in the local office.

Once, while at lunch with a client, Ann learned confidentially about a client issue that was extremely important to the firm. She was conflicted by her loyalty to her client friend who had disclosed the information and the firm she loved so much.

Ann's solution was to counsel with an experienced female partner she had grown very close to through the MS All-Stars activities. The trusted Partner proposed a clever plan Ann had not thought of which created a "win-win" between the firm and its client. The solution enabled Ann to honor all her relationships. In a way, her trusted relationships within the firm were KEY to Ann becoming a hero of sorts in the local office. The Partners did not soon forget her contribution in saving this client.

KEY Questions:

1. What types of people did Ann have access to at this time?

2. Who did Ann connect with and what did she do to connect with them?

3. What was her cost of networking, e.g. time, money, opportunity costs, etc.?

4. What were the benefits of networking, e.g., tangible, intangible, monetary, ideas, information, etc.?

5. Besides Ann, who was actively networking in the story? What did they do? How did they benefit?

6. Who are the good networkers where you are? What can you do better to connect with people where you are now? What is stopping you from accessing the Key?

The Full Benefits of Networking

•   •   •

Networking is Key to a fulfilling and successful career. By the time the benefits really kick in, networking is habitual and the results seem magical. Carl Jung defined synchronicity as "a meaningful coincidence of two or more events, where something other than the probability of chance is involved." Relationships are that "other than chance." Over time, there is no doubt consistent networking creates synchronicity. Help and opportunity come from places no one would have ever considered possible.

•   •   •

In her ninth year at the firm, Ann received a call from the National Office. One of the people she had been working with for years on the MS All-Stars team wanted to talk to her about a new career opportunity. Ann loved the fact that once again, her network was looking out for her.

The firm needed a successful leader for an ex-patriot assignment in the regional headquarters in Taipei, Taiwan. The firm was beginning to land very large and important clients in Taiwan, and with "China rising" they expected explosive growth in the region in the near future. Unfortunately, at that time, communications and coordination between the US headquarters and the Taipei office was woeful and clients were beginning to complain.

The selection committee had considered several experienced partners for the position, but just couldn't find one with the right combination of technical skills, communications abilities, relationship building talent, and cultural sensitivity. When Ann's name was mentioned at the planning committee meeting, the chairman's face lit up. He had recruited Ann to the firm 8 years ago and was following her career.

Interestingly, her parents' networks would also be KEY to getting up to speed quickly on the job.

He liked her success in the firm and remembered she grew up in Taiwan and also had a minor in International Business and Asian Studies. He thought she was the best choice even though she was neither the best accountant nor the most experienced candidate. With enthusiasm he commented, "I sure am glad Ann and I stayed in touch all these years!" He didn't stay in touch, Ann did, but who cares? Ann would be perfect for the job.

Big-4 international ex-patriot assignments are a plum. Ann was offered a promotion with a higher salary paid in US dollars and tax equalization. She would be given two trips per year back to the US for her and her husband. They would also get a housing allowance, and a car and driver. Given Ann's grandparents were getting older so a 2-3 year stay in Taiwan would be fantastic and the career challenges would be good as well. Ann accepted the position and her husband won a job teaching English during the day and went to night school to learn Mandarin.

By this time, Ann had real skills in relationship building and networking. She also knew a bit about some of the intercultural issues impeding the relationship between Taiwan and the USA. Oddly enough, her parents' networks would also be KEY to getting her up to speed quickly in her new job.

Ann's father had been an executive with the Evergreen Corporation in Taipei before taking a move to become the

USA CEO of a Taiwanese computer manufacturer. Taiwan is small and like most successful executives he knew many successful business leaders in Taipei and across Asia. What's more, he was a classmate of the Firm's Office Managing Partner at Taiwan National University in the 1980s. Because of this long-time relationship Ann had an instant mentor and ally in the Taipei office – namely her boss. It truly is a small world.

It truly is a small world.

Ann knew an international move like this would impact her relationships, "out of sight out of mind." So, as soon as she accepted the promotion she began to envision the announcement email and the ways she could stay in touch with her network from off-shore. By now, making an announcement to her network was like clockwork and most of her contacts responded with encouragement and best wishes.

This time, however, since she was moving far away and staying connected would be tougher and more important than ever, Ann added three requests to the bottom of her e-mail note:

1. Please send me your mailing address

2. What is the month and day of your birthday?

3. Please look for my invitation to connect on LinkedIn.

In Taiwan, Ann would have an administrative assistant. Ken Tudhope had always encouraged her to send birthday cards, but she never could find the time ("How did he do it?" she thought when she received his card each year.). Now, with an administrative assistant she could send birthday cards. The replies came pouring in and Ann soon had a solid birthday card list with good mailing addresses. That year her contacts received: a birthday card, and a red card on the Chinese New Year (different type of holiday card).

Consistently updating him on her career progress was KEY to them feeling like old friends when she called.

She linked with 90% of her network on LinkedIn and was able to effectively stay in touch from a distance. One year, she challenged her network to support her MS ride like never before; if they committed to $10,000 in total donations, she would return from Asia to ride. Her network came through by exceeding the goal. She came back and completed the ride on a borrowed bike (there were many offers). The weekend was a blast with old friends, colleagues, and long-time MS All-Stars teammates. She used the weekend activities and long ride (6 hours) to reconnect with the Southern California management and get an update on business issues and office politics.

She was certainly well positioned for success with supporters locally, nationally, and internationally.

Needless to say, Ann was able to get up to speed quickly in her new job using her networking skills and contacts on both sides of the Pacific. When she realized the staff in Taipei had little knowledge of US GAAP, were culturally limited and weak in English, she made a call to Dr. Tang. The fact they had spoken a few times at BAP recruiting events, and Ann consistently updating him on her career progress was KEY to them feeling like old friends when she called. Dr. Tang mentioned he was so glad "they had stayed in touch."

Ann knew that with the financial woes in the State of California, her university had been accepting more high-tuition international students. She asked Dr. Tang if there were any top students with Chinese language skills graduating soon and planning to return to Asia. The answer was yes. With Dr. Tang's help, Ann recruited three top candidates from the Masters in Accounting program. This cadre was a first for the Taipei office and made a significant difference in the short run. It also started a unique recruiting relationship that had a significant positive impact on the firm's Taipei office for many years into the future.

Ann had plenty of job opportunities both inside and outside the firm when she returned to California. Soon she would be considered for the Partnership and she was certainly well positioned for success with supporters locally, nationally and internationally. With so many close friends in the firm she was confident a partnership offer would be forthcoming, but her networking efforts gave her ample job opportunities outside the firm so her bases were well covered.

At about this time Ann was selected for a position on the firm's diversity council. When asked about her success and what the firm could do to assist women, minorities and others to be prepared for executive positions in the firm, she said, "Networking is the KEY." Ann introduced Ken to the council and he was paid extremely well to deliver 5 day-long workshops teaching professional networking to regional leadership throughout the world. Funny, all Ken did, really, was tell Ann's story.

Over the years Ann's connections had generated significant financial capital for her career.

While Ann didn't implement the 5 steps to networking for new professionals (see Appendix - 1 or go to www.thekey.com) exactly like Ken recommends, she did what she could and became an excellent networker. $50 per connection...who knows? No doubt, however, over the years Ann's connections had generated significant financial capital for her career. It ultimately helped her be invited into the Partnership. Networking and relationship building are different for everyone, but like Harvey Mackay says in his excellent book *Dig Your Well Before You're Thirsty*, "Networking is like getting dressed, it doesn't so much matter how you do it, what's important is that you do it."

Key Questions:

1. What types of people did Ann have access to at this time?

2. Who did Ann connect with and what did she do to connect with them?

3. What was her cost of networking, e.g. time, money, opportunity costs, etc.?

4. What were the benefits of networking, e.g., tangible, intangible, monetary, ideas, information, etc.?

5. Besides Ann, who was actively networking in the story? What did they do? How did they benefit?

6. Who are the good networkers where you are? What can you do better to connect with people where you are now? What is stopping you from accessing the Key?

About the Author

Ken Tudhope may very well know more people working in Finance & Accounting jobs in Orange County than any other person. He has boundless energy for networking and is actively involved in many Orange County professional associations in Finance & Accounting. He is author of Tudhope's Networking Notes, a collection of short articles, audio blogs and You Tube videos on the subject of networking (www.networkingnote.com). Tudhope's Networking Notes are published in the monthly newsletter of the Orange County chapter of Finance Executives International (FEI), on the CorpFinCafe.com blog, and in the monthly networking newsletter InContact Finance.

- ✓ Institute of Management Accountants (IMA) – Past President, Board Member
- ✓ Financial Executives International (FEI) – Past President, Board Member, Membership Chair receiving the world-wide Award for Membership Growth both in 2006 & 2007

- ✓ UCLA Anderson School Alumni Association - Board Member, Career Services Chair
- ✓ American Electronics Association (AEA) - Past member of the CFO Committee
- ✓ Harvard Business School Alumni Association - Past Keynote Speaker
- ✓ OC | CFO Network – Founder & ongoing sponsor
- ✓ International Professionals in Finance and Accounting, Co-Founder
- ✓ Executive Finance Forums – Founder & sponsor
- ✓ OC Excel User Group – Co-Founder
- ✓ Frequent keynote speaker at businesses, universities, and civic groups
- ✓ Scoutmaster Irvine Boy Scout Troop 645

Reach Ken at (949)439-9457 or ktudhope@projectpro.net

About Project Pro Search

Founded in 2007, Project Pro Search is a boutique executive search firm focused on professional and executive level positions in finance and accounting in Orange County, California. The firm's value proposition: "Connected. So We Can Connect You." speaks to both clients looking to hire the best talent and candidates looking for quality employment. Unique because we know so many people, and more often than not, have personal and confidential knowledge about the people we present. Our large, multi-national competitors simply cannot provide that service. If you are hiring in finance and accounting in Orange County, please call Project Pro Search at (949)336-7555 or go to www.projectpro.net.

Epilog

During the editing process for *The Key* several people asked me if I really wanted to be a character in my own book. They were concerned that it was confusing and a bit self-serving.

I kept my name in the book for three reasons: first, my work as a speaker at the local universities has a real impact on people. It's my way of giving back and I want to encourage others join me in supporting the young people in our profession. My passion for networking is changing attitudes and I don't know of another person who does what I do. Ann could be any number of students or recent graduates who have heard me speak and I've mentored in the area of networking.

Second, this is a self-published book used to promote my company and my brand as the preeminent networker in Finance and Accounting in Orange County California. As a small business owner I have to use every opportunity I have to further my brand and my company; what better way than to be a character in my own book?

Third, and most importantly, I want to show my readers that I practice what I preach. The benefits of networking are for everyone, including me. Just like my readers, I need to be constantly investing in social capital. In fact, as a professional recruiter it can be argued that I need to network more than most. My company's value position: "Connected. So We Can Connect You." speaks to both the clients that pay us to find great candidates and the candidates who win great jobs through our searches.

I add value and earn a living because it's easier and faster for people to access my network, than it is for them to build a network of their own. I have a comparative advantage vis-à-vis my competition, because I simply have a bigger network of contacts than they do. How do I do it? Exactly the same way Ann does: "Give first, give often, expect nothing."

For years I have taken time to go to the local universities to deliver networking speeches to the students. This is a clear example of giving first as I have never taken a penny for my time and clients don't pay recruiters to find entry level people when they can get all they'd like at the university career center. I do it because I have a passion for networking and see the real benefit and opportunity for the fresh faces in the crowd. If education is the great equalizer, networking is a close second.

While my work with the university students is a gift to them, there is definitely value in it for me. I believe I'm planting seeds. Once again, I am setting an example because networking takes time. I absolutely believe there is no short cut to success through networking. The students will become viable candidates in 5-7 years and, in 10-15 years; a few of them will become prospects.

The difference between me and many others in my profession is that when I call these students turned prospects in 5 or 10 years, my call will not be a cold call. My plan is to have a build a relationship with them which starts with a talk at Beta Alpha Psi when they were still in school and continues with an internet relationship through my blog, tweets, and networking list (InContact), and now my book. I will always be *the guy* in the book who used to come to school and rant about networking!

Appendix – 1

6 Key Steps: A Simple Networking Plan for New Professionals

"More business decisions occur over lunch and dinner than any other time, and yet no MBA courses are given on the subject."

-Peter Drucker

The following is a simple networking system developed specifically for new professionals, but equally valuable for people at all levels. Each activity is simple, low-cost and available to everyone. The proposed networking activities will not only help you to accumulate valuable social capital now, but will also instill useful networking habits that will be retained for a lifetime.

The steps are in order of importance so be sure to make significant progress on each step before moving on to the next. Be both persistent and patient, as it will take most new professionals 12 to 18 months to make solid progress on all five steps. Building solid relationships is a gradual process that has no shortcuts.

Key # 1 is to obtain, record and protect the contact information for the people you meet in business. You will need to buy BOTH a business card scanner and a Rolodex® file with a combined cost of less than $100. Start collecting, scanning, filing and DISPLAYING business cards from the people you meet. Use social media, but understand that at this point it is too new and uncertain to trust as the only source of recording contact information. Your company will have a CRM, but the information in it belongs to the company and you never know how long you will stay or how abruptly you will depart. Never confuse your network with your company's network.

Your Cardscan® scanner will be easy to use and will connect easily to any personal computer and syncs to all contact management systems. The optical character recognition (OCR) capability automatically scans and then picks up and records contact information which means you will **not** have to manually enter this information. After each business card is scanned, the software allows you to confirm it is correct and then stores it in MS Outlook, Act!, Google, or any other contact system. As the names go into the system add any noteworthy information that will help you remember the person, e.g., where you met them, what they look like, interests, contacts in common, etc.

Once scanned, each business card is stapled to a Rolodex® card and placed in the Rolodex® file. Always keep the Rolodex® with the cards displayed on top of your desk – "front and center." It will remind you of the value of networking and make an impression on your colleagues and visitors when they see it. Managers and executives know the value of connections, and your Rolodex® will signal to them that you too have learned this lesson and are ahead of your peers. These contacts will be of significant value to you and your employer.

Yes, in the era of LinkedIn, Facebook, Google and other social networking and contact management applications, I am recommending using a Rolodex® business card file. While social media and other contact management applications are very useful and efficient, professional relationships usually start with a business card. This is why everyone carries one and why you need to collect them.

KEY Checklist # 1

1. Buy and install a contact Management System. We recommend MS Outlook.

2. Buy and install an OCR card scanner. Link it to your contact software.

3. Buy a Rolodex® File and put it on your desk "front and center."

4. Establish a weekly business card goal. Remember, consistent growth is more important than quantity.

Key **# 2** is to send 1 or 2 announcement e-mails out per year. Think of this as the "Christmas Letter" for business. Announce promotions, awards, contributions, certifications, moves, company information, publications, etc. Bcc or mail merge e-mail is best and include everyone on your contact list. This information will remind people about you: where you are, and what you are up to in your career. For this communication "less is more," so keep your messages brief.

There is a self-promotion aspect to this communication that is quite appropriate, but can be touchy for some people so keep the message "all business." Also conclude with a request for an update from your contacts. If and when people respond ALWAYS reply with a personal message and record any changes to their situation and / or contact information.

KEY Checklist # 2

1. Maintain a list of noteworthy items you can announce.

2. If you have trouble with this list, what does this say about your career progression?

Key # 3 Increase the size and diversity of your network by volunteering. The best example is the corporate United Way campaign, but any volunteer activity will suffice. Company executives tend to lead these activities so it may very well be your best bet for early access to managers and executives who are key decision makers in your company. You will also meet new people outside your company. Simply attending these events won't increase your relationships; you've got to get involved. Treat it like a paid job and put in serious effort. When you do a great job, the people you meet will appreciate your contribution and remember you as a person of quality.

KEY Checklist # 3

1. Select a volunteer group that you believe in that is associated with your job or profession.

2. Decide to get involved.

3. Get contact information for all involved. Follow-up with executives and people who made large contributions

Key **# 4** is to join Toastmasters International. Toastmasters© is the most cost effective self-development program on earth and a great place to learn how to network through groups. To successfully network through groups you must **sign up, show up, follow up and step up** (See a discussion of networking through groups in Appendix - 2) and Toastmasters gives you the opportunity for all four.

At Toastmasters, you will gain confidence, connections and empathy; all personal skills you will need as your career progresses. Chapters are everywhere, and the cost is very low; pick one, sign up, show up consistently, follow up by obtaining and recording contact information of your fellow members, and step up into leadership when the time is right.

KEY Checklist # 4

1. What is the expected cost in time and money versus the expected benefit? Join now, do not wait.

2. What meeting time and location works best?

3. Attend a meeting as a guest.

4. Join and commit to 6 months.

Key # 5 is to use your current contacts to meet and build relationships with noteworthy people. This will increase your confidence and expose you to targeted networking. Use your closest family members and friends to get introduced to four executives or otherwise noteworthy people in your geographic area.

Don't settle; target people who are important, busy and otherwise difficult to get access to. Whether you like it or not, your parents are a great source of introductions and may very well be your best referral source; use them. If not your parents, approach others that you know well and trust such as pastors, professors, coaches, or neighbors.

Get four introductions, arrange appointments over the next year, meet with them, ask for their advice and stay in touch forever. Hopefully some of these people will develop into advisors and mentors. Depending on their background, they may be able to directly benefit your career.

<u>KEY Checklist # 5</u>

1. List four noteworthy people you want to meet:
   _____, _____, _____, _____

2. Ask your network for introductions to these people

3. Stay in contact with them for the long haul, announcements, birthday cards, holiday cards, lunches, etc.

Key #6 is to send out **hand-written** cards. This will not only help you stay in contact with the people you meet in the first 4 steps, but will also be a unique thing for you to do to make a positive impression on your contacts. Few people do it anymore, so the people receiving your cards will appreciate the effort and maintain a positive impression about you. This will give you a reason to personally touch people in your network at least two times per year on birthdays and at the holidays. If you don't want to ask for birthdays, then purchase a few packages of thank-you cards and start sending them out. If you can't think of what to be thankful for, buy a copy of John Kralick's excellent book "365 Thank Yous: The Year a Simple Act of Daily Gratitude Changed My Life."

KEY Checklist # 6

1. Purchase blank greeting cards.

2. Find 25 birthdays and add them to Outlook.

3. One thank-you card sent per week. Read Kralik's book.

I guarantee if you practice these 6 activities, you will stand out among your peers and develop valuable professional skills. Also, you will build meaningful relationships that will last a lifetime.

So much of the self-development and business literature is focused on activities and techniques that are primarily useful to mid-career professionals or executives, and often require position, title, budgets and decision making authority.

The great thing about this simple 6-step networking plan is that it is an individual activity that is just as beneficial to a new professional as it is to the CEO of an organization. Start networking now.

Appendix - 2:

Networking Through Groups

While "networking is definitely not an event," groups are a fantastic when to build a network. The group provides a context to get together and usually involves a common interest, e.g., professional society, alumni group, industry association, etc. What's more, they normally have a directory with contact information and pictures and background information for all members.

Networking through groups is actually very simple. I've broken it down into four easy steps, and if you follow these consistently over time you will be amazed at how you can enrich your networking activities and build your relationships.

If you are reading "The Key" you might have already taken the first step by Signing Up for a networking group. There are some people who want to build a network but they don't sign up for any groups and their networks don't grow. Good for you!

Next, you'll need to Show Up. Do you attend each and every meeting? If not, you should. The more you go, the more you know. There are many networkers that simply don't come to the meetings. They confuse Jeffery's Gitomer's "50 Butt Rule" - if there are 50 butts in a room, his butt is there too - with their own 50 buts. They say, "I would have come, but... I tried to make it, but...I thought about it but...but...but...but...but...but...but...but...but..."

Next, you have to Follow Up. After the meeting, connect with a few of the people you meet in some way or other. Send an e-mail, call on the phone, or drop by in person, anything to cement the connection that was begun at the meeting. You will be in an exclusive group, because so few people follow up. No doubt you will be appreciated and remembered for it. Those who don't follow up will have to reintroduce themselves to the same people over and over, meeting after meeting.

Finally, Step Up. By working side-by-side with others in the group you will deepen the connections that you have already created by consistently attending meeting and events. Usually this starts a committee position or event chairmanship, and then evolves into a board seat or officer role, but it doesn't have to. Heck, you could do something crazy like volunteer to write a column on networking in the Association's newsletter like I did for FEI- Orange County six years ago! If you do, many people will see your name and you will add to your network of contacts.

About BETA APLHA PSI

[reprinted from the Beta Alpha Psi website]

OBJECTIVES

BETA ALPHA PSI is an honorary organization for Financial Information students and professionals. The primary objective of Beta Alpha Psi is to encourage and give recognition to scholastic and professional excellence in the business information field. This includes promoting the study and practice of accounting, finance and information systems; providing opportunities for self-development, service and association among members and practicing professionals, and encouraging a sense of ethical, social, and public responsibility.

Beta Alpha Psi was founded in 1919. By 2012, there will be 296 chapters on college and university campuses with over 300,000 members initiated since Beta Alpha Psi's formation.

MEMBERSHIP

Membership in Beta Alpha Psi includes those persons of good moral character who have achieved scholastic and/or professional excellence in the fields of accounting, finance, or information systems, who have been initiated by an existing chapter and who remain in good standing.

Minimum scholastic requirements for undergraduate membership are set forth in the by-laws. Graduate student initiates must have been accepted and matriculated into a master's degree level program. Individual chapters may establish higher admission criteria.

ORGANIZATION

Beta Alpha Psi is governed by a constitution and bylaws. The governing body is the Board of Directors. The Board consists of thirteen financial information professionals or professors of Accounting, Finance or Information Systems, the chair of the International Advisory Forum, and two alumni representatives. The alumni representatives are chosen from recent graduates who were active in Beta Alpha Psi chapters.

THE INTERNATIONAL ADVISORY FORUM

The Forum is comprised of prominent professionals who are active in professional service and consulting firms, industry, and government. The members serve three-year terms. The Forum provides the Board of Directors external advice and assistance in both regular operations and special projects of Beta Alpha Psi.

THE INTERNATIONAL CHAPTER

The International Chapter is comprised of all Faculty Advisors, student presidents, and past and present officers of Beta Alpha Psi. This body holds an annual meeting and banquet in August and provides advice and assistance to the Board of Directors.

LOCAL CHAPTERS

Local Chapters are comprised of student and faculty members at each school. Student officers guide the chapter's operations and activities, supervised by the Faculty Advisors. Beta Alpha Psi is a tax-exempt organization under Section 501(c)(3) of the Internal

Revenue Code. Contributions to Beta Alpha Psi and its local chapters are deductible.

FUNDING

Beta Alpha Psi gains a portion of its annual budget from a charter maintenance fee and a one-time initiation fee. Although there are other minor revenues from royalties and interest on investments, the bulk of the receipts come from contributions from industry, consulting and professional service firms.

In 1982, the Associates Program was initiated. Through the Associates, industrial, consulting and professional service firms contribute to Beta Alpha Psi activities.

ACTIVITIES

The Board establishes a program for chapter activities to serve as a guide and incentive for chapter competition. The goal of chapter activities is to involve all members fully in chapter affairs. SUCCESSFUL CHAPTER OPERATION REQUIRES PARTICIPATION BY MOST MEMBERS IN ATTENDING MEETINGS, SERVING ON COMMITTEES,

PARTICIPATING IN ACTIVITIES, AND STRIVING FOR ACADEMIC EXCELLENCE.

All chapters are evaluated annually on their service to members, campus, community, and profession. Superior chapters are recognized each year at the Beta Alpha Psi's annual meeting.

Chapter activities are divided into categories according to: plan of activities and budget, initiations, professional programs, involvement in campus and professional activities, community service, and annual year-end report. Activities include speeches and panel discussions by students, faculty and professionals; field trips; business meetings; and a wide variety of professional, social, and service activities.

Employers of accounting, finance and information systems students are familiar with Beta Alpha Psi and its activities. It is understood that Beta Alpha Psi represents excellence and that its activities are designed to supplement a student's education.

The activities of student members include:

- ✓ Attendance at chapter meetings, socials, and recruiting events,
- ✓ Attendance at regional meetings, and
- ✓ Attendance and participation at the annual meeting.

INSIGNIA

The emblem of Beta Alpha Psi denotes the promise of careers for financial information professionals. The rising sun signifies these professional positions as rising ever higher among economic activities. The crossed keys symbolize knowledge as a means of opening the doors of the financial world. The letters Beta, Alpha, and Psi denote scholarship, social responsibility, and practicality, respectively.

Made in the USA
Charleston, SC
06 March 2013